© Little Book Publishing LLC
2022

Do you ask yourself these questions?

What is wrong with me?

Why don't things seem to be working out for me?

Why am I alone?

Why does no one love me?

This is the book to read to get yourself unto a new life.

The book has 6 steps to start making the changes you need to improve your life's journey. So, let's begin.

Step 1. Understand the problems in your life.

First it is important to recognize what you feel is holding you back. What seems to be the problem? Why don't things seem to be getting better with time?

Take a moment to make a list. Be sure to include all the things that you recognize needs to change.

Think about anything you feel is a setback for you in your life. Is there something stopping you from your happiness in life? This list should contain anything that you feel needs improvement even if it is just working on your attitude, or better work habits. This list should contain the most important factors for your life even if they may seem small to someone else. What situations or events have impacted your life so much that it has caused you to change your lifestyle and have caused you to struggle. Write down anything that you feel is blocking you from where you want to be in your life.

Think back to when or even where your life seemed to change for the worst. What time of the day was it? Who was around? What was the environment like? What was your current state of mind?

Living in the past isn't good but understanding it and growing from it will be a step in the right direction. I am not here to preach religion to anyone or force my own beliefs unto you. For that would defeat the whole point of this book. I will say that I am a follower of Christ, but it is not my place to judge or to force anyone to believe in what I do.

I am only here to share my experiences and growth with others, hoping to make a difference in the lives of many. I truly believe when God said, "feed my sheep," he meant with knowledge.

I don't want this list to take up too much of your time although, the list may be lengthy for some of you.

Once you have completed the list then put it away. It is important that you do not focus on the list. Keep the list for later in a safe place to refer back to it.

Finding the start of what has caused you to lose focus in the 1st place is important for fixing the problem later. If you don't feel there ever was a problem to begin with then that may very well be part of the problem.

Sometimes, it is hard for one to recognize that there was even a problem to begin with. Maybe you are living the dream that you have heard so much about and yet you still feel something is missing.

All these feelings need to be recognized in this first step. What could it be that is still missing, which is causing you to have a void in your life?

Understand that each individual will have a different area in life that will be more profound than your peers, but most people in life essentially want the same thing. Most people want to have a purpose in life, want to be loved, and want to enjoy life with a sense of peace in their hearts.

At this time, you should have established a timeline for the events in your life. By now I am sure you have already been overthinking your current situations. This may have become frustrating just thinking about it all. Now, let us change the focus by entering the second step of meditation.

Step 2. Meditation

Meditation is often used to clear the mind. So now, I want you to do a simple exercise to take some tension off your brain. I am sure you have heard of this method many of times before, so this isn't something new.

Simply close your eyes and imagine what kind of life you would want to have. Think about the house you would have and who is living with you. Think about what kind of car you would be driving and about how your social life would be. Think about your personal relationships and how they would be. What career would you have?

Be detailed in your thoughts. Let your mind create the imaginable. Relax your whole body while you get lost in this peaceful world you have created. Find your happy place. Someone or something that makes you smile, while you take deep breaths and let your body completely relax.

The second step to recovery is meditation. If you are always tense, then it makes it harder for one to focus on finding a solution. There are all different ways to meditate but for me finding your happy place always works best.

For others meditating may be listening to soothing music or taking a walk. I have also found that reading a book that you like will take your mind from the real world and take you into a place where you are eager to see the outcome of the story. I would hope in time that you will soon become eager to see where your real life is going to take you, so that you will begin to look forward to the next days in your life.

The use of meditation in this simple form is meant to help you refocus and break the pattern of stress. If you can imagine the place you want to be in, then that's what you will have to keep you focused and motived on achieving that goal. Let's move onto step three.

Step 3. Self-care

This is not where I focus on your hygiene but that is definitely a part of self-care. Most people feel they have this area down well which is usually a common misconception. I say this only because this is a part of a healthy life. If things are going in disarray, then maybe you need to reevaluate this area.

So, to define self-care seems simple but let's dig a little deeper. Let's see how many of these you can check off.

1. Hygiene

2. Taking care of your physical body with proper diet and exercise.

3. Taking time out for yourself

4. Learning about yourself

5. Giving yourself encouragement

6. Giving yourself praise

7. Finding ways to better cope with things that cause you dissatisfaction

8. Removing people from your life that cause you harm.

This can mean physically, mentally, emotionally, or all three.

This one is so important and not always easy because these people may be someone you are very close to, or even a co-worker.

Self-care means taking care of yourself in a way that others can see that you aren't going to stand for anything less than how you would treat yourself. If you neglect your body by eating poorly then

others can see your lack of self-control or self - confidence. This then shows them how they can play on your weaknesses, which may very well be food.

If you feel you have mastered this area in your life, then good for you. You are not a pushover. LOL just kidding but this does mean that you understand how important it is to take care of yourself because you only have one body and one life.

Before we move on to step 4, I want to stop and share with you my journey and struggles of knowing my worth and the importance of my life.

I look at myself in the mirror, and I fight to get my peace back. For looking at myself crying only makes me see all the pain I am truly in. I look at myself and I tell myself that I can overcome these thoughts and emotions, for I don't like to see what I look like when I am crying.

Watching myself cry is a turning point for me to find my strength in my weakest moment of despair. I only can regain my awareness when I start focusing on watching myself crying. I said to myself, "I don't like seeing you this way. You can do better, and you will. Not for anyone else but for yourself. You will find peace in the storm, and a spark of hope when things seem hopeless."

It is up to me to redirect my thoughts and emotions. Do

not allow the world to overtake your peace by giving you obstacles and taking away your peace. When craziness begins to happen, it is time to stop and refocus because life has gotten the better of you. In my moment of weakness, and hopelessness I began to rebuild myself. I began telling myself that I needed to calm down and stop crying. I was hurt. For I felt the world wasn't being fair to me and I didn't want to keep doing this. I felt defeated. I said to myself, "was my life only created to be chaotic and confusing?" But when I looked at my eyes again in the mirror, I knew I had to stop and redirect my thoughts. Deep inside of me I knew I was truly a good person who was simply trying to find my inner peace in such a crazy world. I knew life came with many challenges and I am not one that likes to lose. In my weakest moment I saw my strength. It didn't seem like much at the time with all the pain and anger and hurt that sat on top of it, but it was there. Then I slowly began to calm back down and regroup myself. I was living a nightmare that never seemed to end. But looking at myself in the mirror reminded me of where I had been and where I have grown to. I knew I could face another day because I have don't this before. I made it then and I will make it again now. For fear will not conquer me. I do not walk alone. I will not allow my despair to overtake me like a drug of unrest. I will stand strong and fight my battles like any warrior and I will be successful. As long as I am alive then my life is worth living. For if I am living then I cannot truly rest until I die, so why should I give up when I have more life to be lived? I need to survive. I need to understand. I need to find myself. I need to live. Here are some of the things I wrote on my list that were causing my unrest in my life.

1. Unable to make decisions on important topics

2. Scared of losing my mother to death

3. Unable to trust or believe men

4. Unsatisfied, unsuccessful

5. Unable to hear God sometimes

6. Feelings of no longer wanting to be here

7. Tired, lonely

8. Sad, distressed, and confused a lot.

The main thing that I recognized in my list was that I was looking for answers. I wanted to understand how people find peace with themselves even when things aren't going how they planned. I didn't want to keep experiencing this sadness and confusion. I wanted to have success in the things that I tried to achieve and be able to stay away from the state of mind where I didn't want to live anymore. I know life is a gift and I didn't want to lose such a precious gift.

Just some things to remember before moving forward in this book. Always take the time to remember what it is that you want out of your life. Then take the time to remove all the negative things that are clouding you from seeing that goal met. Regroup and refocus on your life. Taking this time will truly make a difference. Now let's move on to step four.

Step 4. Forgive

Whatever bad things have happened in your past forgive the people that have made those poor choices to bring unwanted happiness in your life. Just say this to yourself as often as needed, "I am still alive, so I need to keep on living."

This I can speak on from my own experience. I was in my 2nd marriage that ended due to infidelity. He had left for another woman. When my husband left me and my children on Christmas eve I was just devastated. My emotions went from hurt, to anger, to blaming myself, to these total melt downs of crying. I never thought I would be able to get over what had happened. I tried so hard to get him back because I was still so very much in love.

But all of those feelings stopped me from living. I just wanted to crawl in a hole and die. I couldn't forgive him, which made me carry such anger and bitterness throughout my day to day.

Each day I would go through all these emotions over and over again. The feelings of anger, hurt, loneliness, unworthy of love, and so on. The cycle just kept repeating itself. Then one night laying in my bed praying to God. He says to me, "forgive him." I immediately said, "what!" I can't forgive him. I actually laughed. I know that's the Christian thing to do God, but I can't do it. Maybe on my death bed.

Then I continued this conversation with God as if I

had the upper hand and knew what was best. This man did all these things to me and all I was trying to do was love him. Unbelievable that he would do this, for his sin is unforgivable.

 If he wants forgiveness, then he had better ask you Lord because I can't. Then I realized that really was the answer to my problem. I am over here drowning in my sorrows while he had moved in with this other woman and isn't at all worried about me.

Not only was I tired physically, but all those feelings were an emotional roller coaster for me, and I couldn't stop the ride. I was holding on to something that I couldn't change, and he had already moved on.

By the end of the night, I was able to forgive him. It took some time, but I did it. Once I had done this, so much weight was lifted from off of my shoulders. I almost felt like a free woman that just got released from prison. I felt an unbelievable overwhelming amount of peace and was able to sleep for the first time in months.

When you let go of things that you can't change but learn from them and gain growth for your future. Then that means you understand that the past will always be the past, but the future holds much greatness.

You should be glad in knowing that sadness won't last but has become an experience in your life that was so profound for you that you learned from this.

Sometimes, you need a real wakeup call and if the event wasn't so memorable then it wouldn't make a difference in your life. Sometimes, it takes someone to mistreat you in order to really understand a part of you that was weak or unsure about in life. This is sometimes a place where one finds an awakening. I simply learned that I didn't love myself as much as I thought, or I would have gotten out of the relationship much sooner.

Remember that life is meant to be lived and no matter how many good times you have there will still be some bad ones. Learn from all experiences so your next days can be full.

This brings me into step five.

Step 5. Forget the past because it has passed.

I don't mean forget what people have done to you or for you but just know that, that time has passed. It is super important to remind yourself to live in the present because anything after that is in the past.

Children are the best example to use because they are slow to anger and quick to forgive. When you were a young child, you had not a care in the world. You played all day till the sun went down just to be able to do it all again the next day.

How many times do we see children that are fighting about something in one moment but quickly forgive and get back to playing again? If we then go and ask them the next day what they were fighting about, they may not even remember.

This is the greatest part about being a child because they are living in the moment. They aren't focused on what has happened or what is to come, but they are only looking at what is in front of them in that present time. If adults could master this skill, then there would be a lot less court cases, divorces, killings, and mental health issues.

People would be more likely to lend a hand for their neighbors and wouldn't have so many negative things to say to one another. Imagine if you had a disagreement with your current neighbor, but then the next day you were back being good neighbors again. Just knowing that things will go back to being peaceful between one another and also knowing that you can still go over and borrow a cup of sugar when needed is priceless.

Children show us how easy the past is to forget or even just how easy it is to move on after the past has passed. The moment they start playing together again their world goes back to a happy place of fun and imagination. Children do not walk around with a chip on their shoulders but live only in that moment. Leave the past in the past and focus on the moment.

Once you have regrouped yourself with the first 5 steps, I need you to start on step six.

Step 6. Start loving yourself again.

This is the most important part of all the steps. Start loving yourself again. I said again because we may have loved ourselves before, but we are starting over and need to stay in tune with ourselves.

Start loving yourself again. By this I mean, be in love with yourself. Yes, I said it. Be in love with yourself. You are great and there is no one like you in the entire world.

Embrace that idea of self-love.

People that love themselves become very successful in life. I am not just implying the idea of success as having money. In the world of a Monk, success is defined by peace and wisdom. For each person success means different things but uncovering yourself is the greatest gift of all.

Life, your life, is the greatest adventure of them all. Live it to the fullest. Don't waste a moment on trying to change things that are out of your control because love will give your life control. It will give it purpose and meaning. The world needs you and that means a lot.

Once you have mastered self-love then you can share love. For all of the people that have had many broken loves, it is only because you didn't love yourself first. I hear guys say this line too much. "I love you more than I love myself." Well, how can that be? For if you don't love yourself then why should I?

How can you love when you don't know how to love yourself?

How can you say you love yourself, but you have an addiction that is causing you more harm than help and claim to love?

Love starts with you. No one wants to fix a broken heart but be accepted by one that knows what love is and how to provide it without pain. For love is not painful. People that do not know how to love make love look painful. They make love look like it is work.

Loving anyone is not work but being yourself an individual like no other will surely cause disagreements with anyone else who isn't exactly the same as you. A lot of people say it was easier years ago. They look at their grandparents that have been married 50 years. Relationships can last with love.

The best example I can give is from being a parent. My children have done a great many things that hurt me to see them do, but I still love them no matter what (unconditional). Now if the child is causing me physical harm, then I may not be in their presence, but I would still love them from afar. As parents we often say a lot of things but if anything, ever happened to our children we would feel a great loss because our love for them is great. When you saw your baby for the 1st time you were so happy in love. There was no work needed in that moment of love. There was no feeling that made you feel like loving this new baby was work. The work comes from caring for the child and making sure their needs are met but all of those things are different from the feeling of love. The amount of work you put in for caring for that child is based on the amount of love you decide to give to that child. No matter how the children turn out is based off of your love for that child.

Also, as a side note. Parents stop blaming yourself for the way your kids turned out.

You did the best you could in those 18 years, and they can either learn from everything or fail from it. It is always their choice to become the person they want to become because you are done raising them. They cannot come back in 20 years and blame you for why they ended up in jail. The decisions they made landed them in the situations that they are in, so let them own up to their own actions. But that's a whole other book.

Love is what gets people together, and love is what keeps them there. So, in conclusion, remember these steps. Go back to your list after at least a month or so later. See if those problems on the paper are still an issue today. If they are, does it bother you now or do you feel more at peace within yourself? Do you feel you have more control over your life?

Repeat the steps as needed. No one said this would be an overnight fix. Learning how to change and sticking to it can always take time. If you are a person that likes to complain, and you begin working on trying not to complain as much. The task of not complaining may start off very simple and you find you are doing well. Then in the next couple of months you find yourself back complaining again. That is okay and a part of life.

Noticing the change means that you are actively aware. This means that now you can recognize and correct the things that are going in disarray for you. Knowing is the first step to change since most people live in denial.

Change in anything is simply that, change, and there is always time for change. Knowing what is going to work for you will simply be, finding the best of you to share with the world. Don't be afraid to be yourself and be proud of who you are. Everyone is great in their own way, and we all contribute something great to this world.

The goal in the end to find that inner peace and to make life more rewarding for you. Make the choice to change. Live in the moment and may your journey through life be great!

www.ingramcontent.com/pod-product-compliance
Lightning Source LLC
Chamberburg PA
CBHW030916080526
44589CB00010B/338